KEATS AT
WENTWORTH PLACE

Poems written December *1818* to September *1820*
by John Keats

London Borough of Camden 1971

Acknowledgements to the late Dorothy Hewlett for her kindness in contributing the introduction and to Keith Wynn for the cover photograph from a copy, at Keats House, of the original oil-painting in the National Portrait Gallery, London.
Reprinted with corrections, 1986

London Borough of Camden Libraries and Arts Department
from
Keats House Wentworth Place Keats Grove Hampstead London NW3 2RR

ISBN 0 901389 07 2

Printed by Camden's Central Print Unit

Matthew Arnold, referring to Keats's own statement 'I think I shall be among the English poets after my death' added 'He is – he is with Shakespeare'. In support of this bold claim Arnold declared: 'No one, save Shakespeare, has in expression quite the fascinating felicity of Keats, his perfection of loveliness'. This verbal felicity, a clarity of expression, forms an integral part of Keats's world-wide appeal, making him perhaps the most dearly loved of all English poets.

In this old House, so jealously conserved, so carefully tended, he wrote the finest of his poems, the great Odes (with the exception of the *Ode to Autumn*, written at Winchester) during what seems a miraculously short space of time, a matter of months. Here they are presented to the reader in chronological order.

On looking through this collection of poems one can marvel, not only at their technical mastery but their range. *The Eve of St. Mark* demonstrates more clearly, I think, than any other poem Keats's ability to use words as if they were new, as new as when 'old Chaucer used to sing'. There is the clean bright quality of an illumination. We get something of this quality, though more charged with emotion, in the revised portion of *The Fall of Hyperion* written while Keats was savouring the unique quality of Dante in the original. *The Eve of St Mark* Rossetti considered the 'chastest and choicest example of his maturing manner, and shows astonishingly real medievalism in one not bred an artist'. In the same category he placed *La Belle Dame sans Merci*, claiming it as 'the germ from which all the poetry of my group has sprung'. This poem has in its strangeness, however, a richer pulsating quality, working forward to the Odes *to Psyche, on a Grecian Urn, to a Nightingale* and *on Melancholy*; surely the acme of Romantic poetry, great utterances where every rift is loaded with ore.

For full measure we have lighter pieces, such as *Ever let the Fancy roam* and, in graver mood, fine sonnets, two on Fame, the tragic *Why did I laugh tonight?* and *To Sleep* with its lovely closing lines:

> Save me from curious conscience, that still lords
> Its strength for darkness, burrowing like a mole;
> Turn the key deftly in the oiled wards,
> And seal the hushed casket of my soul.

There came a time when Keats's genius, vitiated by disease and frustrated love, could no longer function at full power. Its last manifestation was the accomplished but less inspired *Lamia*, title poem to his 1820 volume, with which he hoped to court a popular favour. A final attempt to woo the general public was a pitiful one, *The Cap and Bells*, which he planned to print under a pseudonym. It aimed at satire with topical hits. This, though there are in it passages both humorous and vivid, has not been considered worthy of inclusion here.

Dorothy Hewlett   November 1970

Contents

Fancy

EVER let the Fancy roam,
Pleasure never is at home:
At a touch sweet Pleasure melteth,
Like to bubbles when rain pelteth;
Then let winged Fancy wander
Through the thought still spread beyond her:
Open wide the mind's cage-door,
She'll dart forth, and cloudward soar.
O sweet Fancy! let her loose;
Summer's joys are spoilt by use,
And the enjoying of the Spring
Fades as does its blossoming;
Autumn's red-lipp'd fruitage too,
Blushing through the mist and dew,
Cloys with tasting: What do then?
Sit thee by the ingle, when
The sear faggot blazes bright,
Spirit of a winter's night;
When the soundless earth is muffled,
And the caked snow is shuffled
From the ploughboy's heavy shoon;
When the Night doth meet the Noon
In a dark conspiracy
To banish Even from her sky.
Sit thee there, and send abroad,
With a mind self-overaw'd,
Fancy, high-commission'd:——send her!
She has vassals to attend her:
She will bring, in spite of frost,
Beauties that the earth hath lost;
She will bring thee, all together,
All delights of summer weather;

All the buds and bells of May,
From dewy sward or thorny spray
All the heaped Autumn's wealth,
With a still, mysterious stealth:
She will mix these pleasures up
Like three fit wines in a cup,
And thou shalt quaff it:——thou shalt hear
Distant harvest-carols clear;
Rustle of the reaped corn;
Sweet birds antheming the morn:
And, in the same moment-hark!
'Tis the early April lark,
Or the rooks, with busy caw,
Foraging for sticks and straw.
Thou shalt, at one glance, behold
The daisy and the marigold;
White-plum'd lilies, and the first
Hedge-grown primrose that hath burst;
Shaded hyacinth, alway
Sapphire queen of the mid-May;
And every leaf, and every flower
Pearled with the self-same shower.
Thou shalt see the field-mouse peep
Meagre from its celled sleep;
And the snake all winter-thin
Cast on sunny bank its skin;
Freckled nest-eggs thou shalt see
Hatching in the hawthorn-tree,
When the hen-bird's wing doth rest
Quiet on her mossy nest;
Then the hurry and alarm
When the bee-hive casts its swarm;

Acorns ripe down-pattering,
While the autumn breezes sing.

Oh, sweet Fancy! let her loose;
Every thing is spoilt by use:
Where's the cheek that doth not fade,
Too much gaz'd at? Where's the maid
Whose lip mature is never new?
Where's the eye, however blue,
Doth not weary? Where's the face
One would meet in every place?
Where's the voice, however soft,
One would hear so very oft?
At a touch sweet Pleasure melteth
Like to bubbles when rain pelteth.
Let, then, winged Fancy find
Thee a mistress to thy mind:
Dulcet-eyed as Ceres' daughter,
Ere the God of Torment taught her
How to frown and how to chide;
With a waist and with a side
White as Hebe's, when her zone
Slipt its golden clasp, and down
Fell her kirtle to her feet,
While she held the goblet sweet,
And Jove grew languid.——Break the mesh
Of the Fancy's silken leash;
Quickly break her prison-string
And such joys as these she'll bring.——
Let the winged Fancy roam
Pleasure never is at home.

Ode

BARDS of Passion and of Mirth,
Ye have left your souls on earth!
Have ye souls in heaven too,
Double-lived in regions new?
Yes, and those of heaven commune
With the spheres of sun and moon;
With the noise of fountains wond'rous,
And the parle of voices thund'rous;
With the whisper of heaven's trees
And one another, in soft ease
Seated on Elysian lawns
Brows'd by none but Dian's fawns
Underneath large blue-bells tented,
Where the daisies are rose-scented,
And the rose herself has got
Perfume which on earth is not;
Where the nightingale doth sing
Not a senseless, tranced thing,
But divine melodious truth;
Philosophic numbers smooth;
Tales and golden histories
Of heaven and its mysteries.

Thus ye live on high, and then
On the earth ye live again;
And the souls ye left behind you
Teach us, here, the way to find you,
Where your other souls are joying,
Never slumber'd, never cloying.

Here, your earth-born souls still speak
To mortals, of their little week;
Of their sorrows and delights;
Of their passions and their spites;
Of their glory and their shame;
What does strengthen and what maim.
Thus ye teach us, every day,
Wisdom, though fled far away.

Bards of Passion and of Mirth,
Ye have left your souls on earth!
Ye have souls in heaven too,
Double-lived in regions new!

Song

I HAD a dove and the sweet dove died;
  And I have thought it died of grieving:
O, what could it grieve for? it was tied,
  With a silken thread of my own hand's weaving;
Sweet little red feet! why did you die——
Why would you leave me, sweet dove! why?
You liv'd all alone on the forest-tree,
Why, pretty thing! could you not live with me?
I kiss'd you oft and gave you white peas;
Why not live sweetly, as in the green trees?

Song

I

HUSH, hush! tread softly! hush, hush, my dear!
All the house is asleep, but we know very well
That the jealous, the jealous old bald-pate may hear,
    Tho' you've padded his night-cap——O sweet Isabel.
    Tho' your feet are more light than a Faery's feet,
    Who dances on bubbles where brooklets meet,——
Hush, hush! soft tiptoe! hush, hush, my dear!
For less than a nothing the jealous can hear.

II

No leaf doth tremble, no ripple is there
    On the river,——all's still, and the night's sleepy eye
Closes up, and forgets all its Lethean care,
    Charm'd to death by the drone of the humming May-fly;
    And the moon, whether prudish or complaisant,
    Has fled to her bower, well knowing I want
No light in the dusk, no torch in the gloom,
But my Isabel's eyes, and her lips pulp'd with bloom.

III

Lift the latch! ah gently! ah tenderly——sweet!
    We are dead if that latchet gives one little clink!
Well done——now those lips, and a flowery seat——
    The old man may sleep, and the planets may wink;
    The shut rose shall dream of our loves and awake
    Full-blown, and such warmth for the morning's take,
The stock-dove shall hatch her soft brace and shall coo,
While I kiss to the melody, aching all through!

The Eve of Saint Mark

UPON a Sabbath-day it fell;
Twice holy was the Sabbath-bell,
That call'd the folk to evening prayer;
The city streets were clean and fair
From wholesome drench of April rains;
And, on the western window panes,
The chilly sunset faintly told
Of unmatured green vallies cold,
Of the green thorny bloomless hedge,
Of rivers new with spring-tide sedge,
Of primroses by shelter'd rills,
And daisies on the aguish hills.
Twice holy was the Sabbath-bell:
The silent streets were crowded well
With staid and pious companies,
Warm from their fire-side orat'ries;
And moving, with demurest air,
To even-song, and vesper prayer.
Each arched porch, and entry low,
Was fill'd with patient folk and slow,
With whispers hush, and shuffling feet,
While play'd the organ loud and sweet.

The bells had ceased, the prayers begun,
And Bertha had not yet half done
A curious volume, patch'd and torn,
That all day long, from earliest morn,
Had taken captive her two eyes,
Among its golden broideries;
Perplex'd her with a thousand things,——
The stars of Heaven, and angels' wings,
Martyrs in a fiery blaze,

Azure saints in silver rays,
Aaron's breastplate, and the seven
Candlesticks John saw in Heaven,
The winged Lion of Saint Mark,
And the Covenantal Ark,
With its many mysteries,
Cherubim and golden mice.

Bertha was a maiden fair,
Dwelling in the old Minster-square;
From her fire-side she could see,
Sidelong, its rich antiquity,
Far as the Bishop's garden-wall;
Where sycamores and elm-trees tall,
Full-leaved, the forest had outstript,
By no sharp north-wind ever nipt,
So shelter'd by the mighty pile.
Bertha arose, and read awhile,
With forehead 'gainst the window-pane.
Again she tried, and then again,
Until the dusk eve left her dark
Upon the legend of St. Mark.
From plaited lawn-frill, fine and thin,
She lifted up her soft warm chin,
With aching neck and swimming eyes,
And dazed with saintly imag'ries.

All was gloom, and silent all,
Save now and then the still foot-fall
Of one returning homewards late,
Past the echoing minster-gate.
The clamorous daws, that all the day

Above tree-tops and towers play,
Pair by pair had gone to rest,
Each in its ancient belfry-nest,
Where asleep they fall betimes,
To music of the drowsy chimes.

All was silent, all was gloom,
Abroad and in the homely room:
Down she sat, poor cheated soul!
And struck a lamp from the dismal coal;
Leaned forward, with bright drooping hair
And slant book, full against the glare.
Her shadow, in uneasy guise,
Hover'd about, a giant size,
On ceiling-beam and old oak chair,
The parrot's cage, and panel square;
And the warm angled winter screen,
On which were many monsters seen,
Call'd doves of Siam, Lima mice,
And legless birds of Paradise,
Macaw, and tender Av'davat,
And silken-furr'd Angora cat.
Untired she read, her shadow still
Glower'd about, as it would fill
The room with wildest forms and shades,
As though some ghostly queen of spades
Had come to mock behind her back,
And dance, and ruffle her garments black.
Untired she read the legend page,
Of holy Mark, from youth to age,
On land, on sea, in pagan chains,
Rejoicing for his many pains.

Sometimes the learned eremite,
With golden star, or dagger bright,
Referr'd to pious poesies
Written in smallest crow-quill size
Beneath the text; and thus the rhyme
Was parcell'd out from time to time:
'Gif ye wol stonden hardie wight——
Amiddes of the blacke night——
Righte in the churche porch, pardie
Ye wol behold a companie
Appouchen thee full dolourouse
For sooth to sain from everich house
Be it in City or village
Wol come the Phantom and image
Of ilka gent and ilka carle
Whom coldè Deathè hath in parle
And wol some day that very year
Touchen with foulè venìme spear
And sadly do them all to die——
Hem all shalt thou see verilie——
And everichon shall by the[e] pass
All who must die that year Alas,
——Als writith he of swevenis,
Men han beforne they wake in bliss,
Whanne that hir friendes thinke hem bound
In crimped shroude farre under grounde;
And how a litling child mote be
A saint er its nativitie,
Gif that the modre (God her blesse!)
Kepen in solitarinesse,
And kissen devoute the holy croce.
Of Goddes love, and Sathan's force,——

He writith; and thinges many mo:
Of swiche thinges I may not show.
Bot I must tellen verilie
Somdel of Saintè Cicilie,
And chieflie what he auctorethe
Of Saintè Markis life and dethe:'

At length her constant eyelids come
Upon the fervent martyrdom;
Then lastly to his holy shrine,
Exalt amid the tapers' shine
At Venice,——

Why Did I Laugh Tonight

WHY did I laugh to-night? No voice will tell:
　No God, no Demon of severe response,
Deigns to reply from Heaven or from Hell.
　Then to my human heart I turn at once.
Heart! Thou and I are here sad and alone;
　I say, why did I laugh? O mortal pain!
O Darkness! Darkness! ever must I moan,
　To question Heaven and Hell and Heart in vain.
Why did I laugh? I know this Being's lease,
　My fancy to its utmost blisses spreads;
Yet would I on this very midnight cease,
　And the world's gaudy ensigns see in shreds;
Verse, Fame, and Beauty are intense indeed,
But Death intenser——Death is Life's high meed.

Hyperion. Book III

THUS in alternate uproar and sad peace,
Amazed were those Titans utterly.
O leave them, Muse! O leave them to their woes;
For thou art weak to sing such tumults dire:
A solitary sorrow best befits
Thy lips, and antheming a lonely grief.
Leave them, O Muse! for thou anon wilt find
Many a fallen old Divinity
Wandering in vain about bewildered shores.
Meantime touch piously the Delphic harp,
And not a wind of heaven but will breathe
In aid soft warble from the Dorian flute;
For lo! 'tis for the Father of all verse.
Flush every thing that hath a vermeil hue,
Let the rose glow intense and warm the air,
And let the clouds of even and of morn
Float in voluptuous fleeces o'er the hills;
Let the red wine within the goblet boil,
Cold as a bubbling well; let faint-lipp'd shells,
On sands, or in great deeps, vermilion turn
Through all their labyrinths; and let the maid
Blush keenly, as with some warm kiss surpris'd.
Chief isle of the embowered Cyclades,
Rejoice, O Delos, with thine olives green,
And poplars, and lawn-shading palms, and beech,
In which the Zephyr breathes the loudest song,
And hazels thick, dark-stemm'd beneath the shade:
Apollo is once more the golden theme!
Where was he, when the Giant of the Sun
Stood bright, amid the sorrow of his peers?
Together had he left his mother fair
And his twin-sister sleeping in their bower,

And in the morning twilight wandered forth
Beside the osiers of a rivulet,
Full ankle-deep in lilies of the vale.
The nightingale had ceas'd, and a few stars
Were lingering in the heavens, while the thrush
Began calm-throated. Throughout all the isle
There was no covert, no retired cave
Unhaunted by the murmurous noise of waves,
Though scarcely heard in many a green recess.
He listen'd, and he wept, and his bright tears
Went trickling down the golden bow he held.
Thus with half-shut suffused eyes he stood,
While from beneath some cumbrous boughs hard by
With solemn step an awful Goddess came,
And there was purport in her looks for him,
Which he with eager guess began to read
Perplex'd, the while melodiously he said:
'How cam'st thou over the unfooted sea?
'Or hath that antique mien and robed form
'Mov'd in these vales invisible till now?
'Sure I have heard those vestments sweeping o'er
'The fallen leaves, when I have sat alone
'In cool mid-forest. Surely I have traced
'The rustle of those ample skirts about
'These grassy solitudes, and seen the flowers
'Lift up their heads, as still the whisper pass'd.
'Goddess! I have beheld those eyes before,
'And their eternal calm, and all that face,
'Or I have dream'd.'——'Yes,' said the supreme shape,
'Thou hast dream'd of me; and awaking up
'Didst find a lyre all golden by thy side,
'Whose strings touch'd by thy fingers, all the vast

'Unwearied ear of the whole universe
'Listen'd in pain and pleasure at the birth
'Of such new tuneful wonder. Is't not strange
'That thou shouldst weep, so gifted? Tell me, youth,
'What sorrow thou canst feel; for I am sad
'When thou dost shed a tear: explain thy griefs
'To one who in this lonely isle hath been
'The watcher of thy sleep and hours of life,
'From the young day when first thy infant hand
'Pluck'd witless the weak flowers, till thine arm
'Could bend that bow heroic to all times.
'Show thy heart's secret to an ancient Power
'Who hath forsaken old and sacred thrones
'For prophecies of thee, and for the sake
'Of loveliness new born. '——Apollo then,
With sudden scrutiny and gloomless eyes,
Thus answer'd, while his white melodious throat
Throbb'd with the syllables.——'Mnemosyne!
'Thy name is on my tongue, I know not how;
'Why should I tell thee what thou so well seest?
'Why should I strive to show what from thy lips
'Would come no mystery? For me, dark, dark,
'And painful vile oblivion seals my eyes:
'I strive to search wherefore I am so sad,
'Until a melancholy numbs my limbs:
'And then upon the grass I sit, and moan,
'Like one who once had wings.——O why should I
'Feel curs'd and thwarted, when the liegeless air
'Yields to my step aspirant? why should I
'Spurn the green turf as hateful to my feet?
'Goddess benign, point forth some unknown thing:
'Are there not other regions than this isle?

'What are the stars? There is the sun, the sun!
'And the most patient brilliance of the moon!
'And stars by thousands! Point me out the way
'To any one particular beauteous star,
'And I will flit into it with my lyre,
'And make its silvery splendour pant with bliss.
'I have heard the cloudy thunder: Where is power?
'Whose hand, whose essence, what divinity
'Makes this alarum in the elements,
'While I here idle listen on the shores
'In fearless yet in aching ignorance?
'O tell me, lonely Goddess, by thy harp,
'That waileth every morn and eventide,
'Tell me why thus I rave, about these groves!
'Mute thou remainest——Mute! yet I can read
'A wondrous lesson in thy silent face:
'Knowledge enormous makes a God of me.
'Names, deeds, gray legends, dire events, rebellions,
'Majesties, sovran voices, agonies,
'Creations and destroyings, all at once
'Pour into the wide hollows of my brain,
'And deify me, as if some blithe wine
'Or bright elixir peerless I had drunk,
'And so become immortal. '——Thus the God,
While his enkindled eyes, with level glance
Beneath his white soft temples, stedfast kept
Trembling with light upon Mnemosyne.
Soon wild commotions shook him, and made flush
All the immortal fairness of his limbs;
Most like the struggle at the gate of death;
Or liker still to one who should take leave
Of pale immortal death, and with a pang

As hot as death's is chill, with fierce convulse
Die into life: so young Apollo anguish'd:
His very hair, his golden tresses famed
Kept undulation round his eager neck.
During the pain Mnemosyne upheld
Her arms as one who prophesied.——At length
Apollo shriek'd;——and lo! from all his limbs
Celestial

[*Unfinished*]

Fairy's Song

SHED no tear——O, shed no tear!
The flower will bloom another year.
Weep no more! O! weep no more!
Young buds sleep in the root's white core.
Dry your eyes! Oh! dry your eyes,
For I was taught in Paradise
To ease my breast of melodies——
        Shed no tear.

Overhead! look overhead!
'Mong the blossoms white and red——
Look up, look up. I flutter now
On this flush pomegranate bough.
See me! 'tis this silvery bill
Ever cures the good man's ill.
Shed no tear! O shed no tear!
The flower will bloom another year.
Adieu, Adieu——I fly, adieu,
I vanish in the heaven's blue——
        Adieu, Adieu!

Faery Song

AH! woe is me! poor Silver-wing!
That I must chaunt thy lady's dirge,
And death to this fair haunt of spring,
Of melody, and streams of flowery verge,——
Poor Silver-wing! ah! woe is me!
That I must see
These blossoms snow upon thy lady's pall!
Go, pretty Page! and in her ear
Whisper that the hour is near!
Softly tell her not to fear
Such calm favonian burial!
Go, pretty Page! and soothly tell,——
The blossoms hang by a melting spell,
And fall they must, ere a star wink thrice
Upon her closed eyes,
That now in vain are weeping their last tears,
At sweet life leaving, and these arbours green,——
Rich dowry from the Spirit of the Spheres,——
Alas! poor Queen!

When They Were Come Into The Faery's Court

WHEN they were come into the Faery's Court
They rang——no one at home——all gone to sport
And dance and kiss and love as faeries do
For Faeries be as humans, lovers true——
Amid the woods they were, so lone and wild,
Where even the Robin feels himself exil'd
And where the very brooks as if afraid
Hurry along to some less magic shade.
'No one at home!' the fretful princess cry'd
'And all for nothing such a dreary ride,
And all for nothing my new diamond cross,
No one to see my Persian feathers toss,
No one to see my Ape, my Dwarf, my Fool,
Or how I pace my Otahaietan mule.
Ape, Dwarf and Fool, why stand you gaping there?
Burst the door open, quick——or I declare
I'll switch you soundly and in pieces tear.'
The Dwarf began to tremble and the Ape
Star'd at the Fool, the Fool was all agape,
The Princess grasp'd her switch, but just in time
The dwarf with piteous face began to rhyme.
'O mighty Princess, did you ne'er hear tell
What your poor servants know but too too well?
Know you the three great crimes in faery land?
The first, alas! poor Dwarf, I understand——
I made a whipstock of a faery's wand——
The next is snoring in their company——
The next, the last, the direst of the three
Is making free when they are not at home
I was a Prince——a baby prince——my doom
You see, I made a whipstock of a wand——

My top has henceforth slept in faery land.
He was a Prince, the Fool, a grown up Prince,
But he has never been a King's son since
He fell a-snoring at a faery Ball——
Your poor Ape was a Prince, and he, poor thing,
Picklock'd a faery's boudoir——now no king,
But ape——so pray your highness stay awhile;
'Tis sooth indeed, we know it to our sorrow——
Persist and _you_ may be an ape tomorrow,——
While the Dwarf spake the Princess all for spite
Peel'd the brown hazel twig to lilly white,
Clench'd her small teeth, and held her lips apart,
Try'd to look unconcern'd with beating heart.
They saw her highness had made up her mind
Quavering like the reeds before the wind,
And they had had it, but ,O happy chance!
The Ape for very fear began to dance
And grin'd as all his ugliness did ache——
She staid her vixen fingers for his sake,
He was so very ugly: then she took
Her pocket mirror and began to look
First at herself and then at him and then
She smil'd at her own beauteous face again.
Yet for all this——for all her pretty face
She took it in her head to see the place.
Women gain little from experience
Either in Lovers, husbands or expence.
'The more the beauty, the more fortune too:
Beauty before the wide world never knew'——
So each Fair reasons, tho' it oft miscarries.
She thought _her_ pretty face would please the faeries,
'My darling Ape I won't whip you today——

Give me the Picklock, sirrah, and go play.'
They all three wept——but counsel was as vain
As crying 'C'up, biddy' to drops of rain.
Yet lingeringly did the sad Ape forth draw
The Picklock from the Pocket in his Jaw.
The Princess took it and dismounting straight
Trip'd in blue silver'd slippers to the gate
And touch'd the wards, the Door full courteously
Opened——she enter'd with her servants three.
Again it clos'd and there was nothing seen
But the Mule grazing on the herbage green.

End of Canto xii

Canto the xiii

The Mule no sooner saw himself alone
Than he prick'd up his Ears——and said 'well done!
At least, unhappy Prince, I may be free——
No more a Princess shall side-saddle me.
O King of Otahaietè——tho' a Mule
"Aye every inch a King"——tho' "Fortune's fool"——
Well done——for by what Mr. Dwarfy said
I would not give a sixpence for her head.'
Even as he spake he trotted in high glee
To the knotty side of an old Pollard tree
And rub'd his sides against the mossed bark

Till his Girths burst and left him naked stark
Except his Bridle——how get rid of that,
Buckled and tied with many a twist and plait?
At last it struck him to pretend to sleep
And then the thievish Monkies down would creep
And filch the unpleasant trammels quite away.
No sooner thought of than adown he lay
Shamm'd a good snore——the Monkey-men descended
And whom they thought to injure they befriended.
They hung his Bridle on a topmost bough
And off he went, run, trot, or any how.

Character of Charles Brown

I

HE is to weet a melancholy carle:
Thin in the waist, with bushy head of hair,
As hath the seeded thistle when in parle
It holds the Zephyr, ere it sendeth fair
Its light balloons into the summer air;
Therto his beard had not begun to bloom,
No brush had touch'd his chin or razor sheer;
No care had touch'd his cheek with mortal doom,
But new he was and bright as scarf from Persian loom.

II

Ne cared he for wine, or half-and-half;
Ne cared he for fish or flesh or fowl,
And sauces held he worthless as the chaff;
He 'sdeigned the swine-head at the wassail-bowl;
Ne with lewd ribbalds sat he cheek by jowl;
Ne with sly lemans in the scorner's chair;
But after water-brooks this Pilgrim's soul
Panted, and all his food was woodland air
Though he would oft-times feast on gilliflowers rare.

III

The slang of cities in no wise he knew,
Tipping the wink to him was heathen Greek;
He sipp'd no olden Tom or ruin blue,
Or nantz or cherry-brandy drank full meek
By many a damsel hoarse and rouge of cheek;
Nor did he know each aged watchman's beat,
Nor in obscured purlieus would he seek
For curled Jewesses, with ankles neat,
Who as they walk abroad make tinkling with their feet.

Sonnet

On A Dream

AS Hermes once took to his feathers light,
   When lulled Argus, baffled, swoon'd and slept,
So on a Delphic reed, my idle spright
   So play'd, so charm'd, so conquer'd, so bereft
The dragon-world of all its hundred eyes;
   And, seeing it asleep, so fled away,
Not to pure Ida with its snow-cold skies,
   Nor unto Tempe, where Jove griev'd that day;
But to that second circle of sad hell,
   Where in the gust, the whirlwind, and the flaw
Of rain and hail-stones, lovers need not tell
   Their sorrows,——pale were the sweet lips I saw,
Pale were the lips I kiss'd, and fair the form
   I floated with, about that melancholy storm.

La Belle Dame Sans Merci

A Ballad

I

O WHAT can ail thee, knight-at-arms,
   Alone and palely loitering?
The sedge has wither'd from the lake,
   And no birds sing.

II

O what can ail thee, knight-at-arms,
   So haggard and so woe-begone?
The squirrel's granary is full,
   And the harvest's done.

III

I see a lilly on thy brow,
   With anguish moist and fever dew,
And on thy cheeks a fading rose
   Fast withereth too.

IV

I met a lady in the meads,
   Full beautiful——a faery's child,
Her hair was long, her foot was light,
   And her eyes were wild.

V

I made a garland for her head,
   And bracelets too, and fragrant zone;
She look'd at me as she did love,
   And made sweet moan.

VI

I set her on my pacing steed,
  And nothing else saw all day long,
Fore sidelong would she bend, and sing
  A faery's song.

VII

She found me roots of relish sweet,
  And honey wild, and manna dew,
And sure in language strange she said——
  'I love thee true'.

VIII

She took me to her elfin grot,
  And there she wept, and sigh'd full sore,
And there I shut her wild wild eyes
  With kisses four.

XI

And there she lulled me asleep,
  And there I dream'd——Ah! woe betide!
The latest dream I ever dream'd
  On the cold hill side.

X

I saw pale kings and princes too,
  Pale warriors, death-pale were they all;
They cried——'La Belle Dame sans Merci
  Hath thee in thrall!'

XI

I saw their starved lips in the gloam,
   With horrid warning gaped wide,
And I awoke and found me here,
   On the cold hill's side.

XII

And this is why I sojourn here,
   Alone and palely loitering,
Though the sedge has wither'd from the lake,
   And no birds sing.

Song of Four Fairies,

Fire, Air, Earth, and Water,
Salamander, Zephyr, Dusketha, and Breama

Salamander HAPPY, happy glowing fire!

Zephyr Fragrant air! delicious light!

Dusketha Let me to my glooms retire!

Breama I to green-weed rivers bright!

Salamander Happy, happy glowing fire!
Dazzling bowers of soft retire,
Ever let my nourish'd wing,
Like a bat's, still wandering,
Faintly fan your fiery spaces,
Spirit sole in deadly places.
In unhaunted roar and blaze,
Open eyes that never daze,
Let me see the myriad shapes
Of men, and beasts, and fish, and apes,
Portray'd in many a fiery den,
And wrought by spumy bitumen.
On the deep intenser roof,
Arched every way aloof,
Let me breathe upon their skies,
And anger their live tapestries;
Free from cold, and every care,
Of chilly rain, and shivering air.

Zephyr Spirit of Fire! away! away!
Or your very roundelay
Will sear my plumage newly budded
From its quilled sheath, all studded
With the self-same dews that fell
On the May-grown Asphodel.
Spirit of Fire——away! away!

Breama Spirit of Fire——away! away!
Zephyr, blue-eyed fairy, turn,
And see my cool sedge-buried urn,
Where it rests its mossy brim
'Mid water-mint and cresses dim;
And the flowers, in sweet troubles,
Lift their eyes above the bubbles,
Like our Queen, when she would please
To sleep, and Oberon will teaze.
Love me, blue-eyed Fairy true,
Soothly I am sick for you.

Zephyr Gentle Breama! by the first
Violet young nature nurst,
I will bathe myself with thee,
So you sometimes follow me
To my home, far, far, in west,
Beyond the nimble-wheeled quest
Of the golden-presenc'd sun:
Come with me, o'er tops of trees,
To my fragrant palaces,
Where they ever floating are
Beneath the cherish of a star
Call'd Vesper, who with silver veil

Ever hides his brilliance pale,
Ever gently-drows'd doth keep
Twilight for the Fayes to sleep.
Fear not that your watery hair
Will thirst in drouthy ringlets there;
Clouds of stored summer rains
Thou shalt taste, before the stains
Of the mountain soil they take,
And too unlucent for thee make.
I love thee, crystal Fairy, true!
Sooth I am as sick for you!

Salamander Out, ye aguish Fairies, out!
Chilly lovers, what a rout
Keep ye with your frozen breath,
Colder than the mortal death.
Adder-eyed Dusketha, speak,
Shall we leave these, and go seek
In the earth's wide entrails old
Couches warm as their's are cold?
O for a fiery gloom and thee,
Dusketha, so enchantingly
Freckle-wing'd and lizard-sided!

Dusketha By thee, Sprite, will I be guided!
I care not for cold or heat;
Frost and flame, or sparks, or sleet,
To my essence are the same;——
But I honour more the flame.
Sprite of Fire, I follow thee
Wheresoever it may be,

To the torrid spouts and fountains,
Underneath earth-quaked mountains;
Or, at thy supreme desire,
Touch the very pulse of fire
With my bare unlidded eyes.

Salamander Sweet Dusketha! paradise!
Off, ye icy Spirits, fly!
Frosty creatures of the sky!

Dusketha Breathe upon them, fiery sprite!

Zephyr and Breama
Away! away to our delight!

Salamander Go, feed on icicles, while we
Bedded in tongued-flames will be.

Dusketha Lead me to those feverous glooms,
Sprite of Fire!

Breama Me to the blooms,
Blue-eyed Zephyr, of those flowers
Far in the west where the May-cloud lowers;
And the beams of still Vesper, when winds are all wist,
Are shed thro' the rain and the milder mist,
And twilight your floating bowers.

Sonnet

To Sleep

O SOFT embalmer of the still midnight,
  Shutting, with careful fingers and benign,
Our gloom-pleas'd eyes, embower'd from the light,
  Enshaded in forgetfulness divine;
O soothest Sleep! if so it please thee, close,
  In midst of this thine hymn, my willing eyes,
Or wait the amen, ere thy poppy throws
  Around my bed its lulling charities;
  Then save me, or the passed day will shine
Upon my pillow, breeding many woes;
  Save me from curious conscience, that still lords
Its strength for darkness, burrowing like a mole;
  Turn the key deftly in the oiled wards,
And seal the hushed casket of my soul.

Sonnet

On Fame

FAME, like a wayward girl, will still be coy
   To those who woo her with too slavish knees,
But makes surrender to some thoughtless boy,
   And dotes the more upon a heart at ease;
She is a Gipsey, will not speak to those
   Who have not learnt to be content without her;
A Jilt, whose ear was never whisper'd close,
   Who thinks they scandal her who talk about her;
A very Gipsey is she, Nilus-born,
   Sister-in-law to jealous Potiphar;
Ye love-sick Bards! repay her scorn for scorn;
   Ye Artists lovelorn! madmen that ye are!
Make your best bow to her and bid adieu,
Then, if she likes it, she will follow you.

Sonnet

On Fame

HOW fever'd is the man, who cannot look
    Upon his mortal days with temperate blood,
Who vexes all the leaves of his life's book,
    And robs his fair name of its maidenhood;
It is as if the rose should pluck herself,
    Or the ripe plum finger its misty bloom,
As if a Naiad, like a meddling elf,
    Should darken her pure grot with muddy gloom:
But the rose leaves herself upon the briar,
    For winds to kiss and grateful bees to feed,
And the ripe plum still wears its dim attire,
    The undisturbed lake has crystal space;
Why then should man, teasing the world for grace,
Spoil his salvation for a fierce miscreed?

Sonnet

IF by dull rhymes our English must be chain'd,
    And, like Andromeda, the Sonnet sweet
Fetter'd, in spite of pained loveliness;
    Let us find out, if we must be constrain'd,
Sandals more interwoven and complete
    To fit the naked foot of poesy:
Let us inspect the lyre, and weigh the stress
    Of every chord, and see what may be gain'd
By ear industrious, and attention meet;
    Misers of sound and syllable, no less
Than Midas of his coinage, let us be
    Jealous of dead leaves in the bay wreath crown;
So, if we may not let the Muse be free,
    She will be bound with garlands of her own.

Ode to Psyche

O GODDESS! hear these tuneless numbers, wrung
  By sweet enforcement and remembrance dear,
And pardon that thy secrets should be sung
  Even into thine own soft-conched ear:
Surely I dreamt to-day, or did I see
  The winged Psyche with awaken'd eyes?
I wander'd in a forest thoughtlessly,
  And, on the sudden, fainting with surprise,
Saw two fair creatures, couched side by side
  In deepest grass, beneath the whisp'ring roof
  Of leaves and trembled blossoms, where there ran
    A brooklet, scarce espied:
'Mid hush'd, cool-rooted flowers, fragrant-eyed,
Blue, silver-white, and budded Tyrian,
They lay calm-breathing on the bedded grass;
  Their arms embraced, and their pinions too;
  Their lips touch'd not, but had not bid adieu,
As if disjoined by soft-handed slumber,
And ready still past kisses to outnumber
  At tender eye-dawn of aurorean love:
    The winged boy I knew;
But who wast thou, O happy, happy dove?
    His Psyche true!

O latest born and lovliest vision far
  Of all Olympus' faded hierarchy!
Fairer than Phoebe's sapphire-region'd star,
  Or Vesper, amorous glow-worm of the sky;

Fairer than these, though temple thou hast none,
    Nor alter heap'd with flowers;
Nor virgin-choir to make delicious moan
    Upon the midnight hours;
No voice, no lute, no pipe, no incense sweet
    From chain-swung censer teeming;
No shrine, no grove, no oracle, no heat
    Of pale-mouth'd prophet dreaming.

O brightest! though too late for antique vows,
    Too, too late for the fond believing lyre,
When holy were the haunted forest boughs,
    Holy the air, the water, and the fire;
Yet even in these days so far retir'd
    From happy pieties, thy lucent fans,
    Fluttering among the faint Olympians,
I see, and sing, by my own eyes inspired.
So let me be thy choir, and make a moan
    Upon the midnight hours;
Thy voice, thy lute, thy pipe, thy incense sweet
    From swinged censer teeming;
Thy shrine, thy grove, thy oracle, thy heat
    Of pale-mouth'd prophet dreaming.

Yes, I will be thy priest, and build a fane
    In some untrodden region of my mind,
Where branched thoughts, new grown with pleasant pain,
    Instead of pines shall murmur in the wind:

Far, far around shall those dark-cluster'd trees
   Fledge the wild-ridged mountains steep by steep;
And there by zephyrs, streams, and birds, and bees,
   The moss-lain Dryads shall be lull'd to sleep;
And in the midst of this wide quietness
A rosy sanctuary will I dress
With the wreath'd trellis of a working brain,
   With buds, and bells, and stars without a name,
With all the gardener Fancy e'er could feign,
   Who breeding flowers, will never breed the same:
And there shall be for thee all soft delight
   That shadowy thought can win,
A bright torch, and a casement ope at night,
   To let the warm Love in!

Two or Three Posies

TWO or three Posies——
With two or three simples——
Two or three Noses——
With two or three pimples——
Two or three wise men——
And two or three ninny's——
Two or three purses——
And two or three guineas——
Two or three raps——
At two or three doors——
Two or three naps——
Of two or three hours——
Two or three Cats——
And two or three mice——
Two or three sprats——
At a very great price——
Two or three sandies——
And two or three tabbies——
Two or three dandies——
And two Mrs —   mum!——
Two or three Smiles——
And two or three frowns——
Two or three Miles——
To two or three towns——
Two or three pegs——
For two or three bonnets——
Two or three dove eggs——
To hatch into sonnets.——

Ode to a Nightingale

I

My heart aches, and a drowsy numbness pains
  My sense, as though of hemlock I had drunk,
Or emptied some dull opiate to the drains
  One minute past, and Lethe-wards had sunk:
'Tis not through envy of thy happy lot,
  But being too happy in thine happiness,——
    That thou, light-winged Dryad of the trees,
      In some melodious plot
Of beechen green, and shadows numberless,
  Singest of summer in full-throated ease.

II

O, for a draught of vintage! that hath been
  Cool'd a long age in the deep-delved earth,
Tasting of Flora and the country green,
  Dance, and Provençal song, and sunburnt mirth!
O for a beaker full of the warm South,
  Full of the true, the blushful Hippocrene,
    With beaded bubbles winking at the brim,
      And purple-stained mouth;
That I might drink, and leave the world unseen,
  And with thee fade away into the forest dim:

III

Fade far away, dissolve, and quite forget
  What thou among the leaves hast never known,
The weariness, the fever, and the fret
  Here, where men sit and hear each other groan;
Where palsy shakes a few, sad, last gray hairs,
  Where youth grows pale, and spectre-thin, and dies;
    Where but to think is to be full of sorrow
      And leaden-eyed despairs,
  Where Beauty cannot keep her lustrous eyes,
    Or new Love pine at them beyond to-morrow.

IV

Away! away! for I will fly to thee,
  Not charioted by Bacchus and his pards,
But on the viewless wings of Poesy,
  Though the dull brain perplexes and retards:
Already with thee! tender is the night,
  And haply the Queen-Moon is on her throne,
    Cluster'd around by all her starry Fays;
      But here there is no light,
  Save what from heaven is with the breezes blown
    Through verdurous glooms and winding mossy ways.

V

I cannot see what flowers are at my feet,
  Nor what soft incense hangs upon the boughs,
But, in embalmed darkness, guess each sweet
  Wherewith the seasonable month endows
The grass, the thicket, and the fruit-tree wild;
  White hawthorn, and the pastoral eglantine;
    Fast fading violets cover'd up in leaves;
      And mid-May's eldest child,
  The coming musk-rose, full of dewy wine,
    The murmurous haunt of flies on summer eves.

VI

Darkling I listen; and, for many a time
  I have been half in love with easeful Death,
Call'd him soft names in many a mused rhyme,
  To take into the air my quiet breath;
Now more than ever seems it rich to die,
  To cease upon the midnight with no pain,
    While thou art pouring forth thy soul abroad
      In such an ecstasy!
  Still wouldst thou sing, and I have ears in vain——
    To thy high requiem become a sod.

VII

Thou wast not born for death, immortal Bird!
　No hungry generations tread thee down;
The voice I hear this passing night was heard
　In ancient days by emperor and clown:
Perhaps the self-same song that found a path
　　Through the sad heart of Ruth, when, sick for home,
　　　She stood in tears amid the alien corn;
　　　　The same that oft-times hath
　Charm'd magic casements, opening on the foam
Of perilous seas, in faery lands forlorn.

VIII

Forlorn! the very word is like a bell
　To toll me back from thee to my sole self!
Adieu! the fancy cannot cheat so well
　As she is fam'd to do, deceiving elf.
Adieu! adieu! thy plaintive anthem fades
　　Past the near meadows, over the still stream,
　　　Up the hill-side; and now 'tis buried deep
　　　　In the next valley-glades:
　Was it a vision, or a waking dream?
　　Fled is that music:——Do I wake or sleep?

Ode on a Grecian Urn

I

THOU still unravish'd bride of quietness,
  Thou foster-child of silence and slow time,
Sylvan historian, who canst thus express
  A flowery tale more sweetly than our rhyme:
What leaf-fring'd legend haunts about thy shape
  Of deities or mortals, or of both,
    In Tempe or the dales of Arcady?
What men or gods are these? What maidens loth?
  What mad pursuit? What struggle to escape?
    What pipes and timbrels? What wild ecstasy?

II

Heard melodies are sweet, but those unheard
  Are sweeter; therefore, ye soft pipes, play on;
Not to the sensual ear, but, more endear'd,
  Pipe to the spirit ditties of no tone:
Fair youth, beneath the trees, thou canst not leave
  Thy song, nor ever can those trees be bare;
    Bold Lover, never, never canst thou kiss,
Though winning near the goal——yet, do not grieve;
  She cannot fade, though thou hast not thy bliss,
    For ever wilt thou love, and she be fair!

III

Ah, happy, happy boughs! that cannot shed
  Your leaves, nor ever bid the Spring adieu;
And, happy melodist, unwearied,
  For ever piping songs for ever new;
More happy love! more happy, happy love!
  For ever warm and still to be enjoy'd,
    For ever panting, and for ever young;
All breathing human passion far above,
  That leaves a heart high-sorrowful and cloy'd,
    A burning forehead, and a parching tongue.

IV

Who are these coming to the sacrifice?
  To what green altar, O mysterious priest,
Lead'st thou that heifer lowing at the skies,
  And all her silken flanks with garlands drest?
What little town by river or sea shore,
  Or mountain-built with peaceful citadel,
    Is emptied of this folk, this pious morn?
And, little town, thy streets for evermore
  Will silent be; and not a soul to tell
    Why thou art desolate, can e'er return.

V

O Attic shape! Fair attitude! with brede
    Of marble men and maidens overwrought,
With forest branches and the trodden weed;
    Thou, silent form, dost tease us out of thought
As doth eternity: Cold Pastoral!
    When old age shall this generation waste,
        Thou shalt remain, in midst of other woe
Than ours, a friend to man, to whom thou say'st,
    Beauty is truth, truth beauty,——that is all
        Ye know on earth, and all ye need to know.

Ode on Melancholy

I

No, no, go not to Lethe, neither twist
  Wolf's-bane, tight-rooted, for its poisonous wine:
Nor suffer thy pale forehead to be kiss'd
  By nightshade, ruby grape of Proserpine;
Make not your rosary of yew-berries,
    Nor let the beetle, nor the death-moth be
      Your mournful Psyche, nor the downy owl
A partner in your sorrow's mysteries;
    For shade to shade will come too drowsily,
      And drown the wakeful anguish of the soul.

II

But when the melancholy fit shall fall
  Sudden from heaven like a weeping cloud,
That fosters the droop-headed flowers all,
  And hides the green hill in an April shroud;
Then glut thy sorrow on a morning rose,
    Or on the rainbow of the salt sand-wave,
      Or on the wealth of globed peonies;
Or if thy mistress some rich anger shows,
    Emprison her soft hand, and let her rave,
      And feed deep, deep upon her peerless eyes.

III

She dwells with Beauty——Beauty that must die;
   And Joy, whose hand is ever at his lips
Bidding adieu; and aching Pleasure nigh,
   Turning to poison while the bee-mouth sips:
Ay, in the very temple of Delight
   Veil'd Melancholy has her sovran shrine,
     Though seen of none save him whose strenuous tongue
Can burst Joy's grape against his palate fine;
   His soul shall taste the sadness of her might,
     And be among her cloudy trophies hung.

Ode on Indolence

I

ONE morn before me were three figures seen,
  With bowed necks, and joined hands, side-faced;
And one behind the other stepp'd serene,
  In placid sandals, and in white robes graced;
They pass'd, like figures on a marble urn,
  When shifted round to see the other side;
    They came again; as when the urn once more
Is shifted round, the first seen shades return;
  And they were strange to me, as may betide
    With vases, to one deep in Phidian lore.

II

How is it, Shadows! that I knew ye not?
  How came ye muffled in so hush a masque?
Was it a silent deep-disguised plot
  To steal away, and leave without a task
My idle days? Ripe was the drowsy hour;
  The blissful cloud of summer-indolence
    Benumb'd my eyes; my pulse grew less and less;
Pain had no sting, and pleasure's wreath no flower:
  O, why did ye not melt, and leave my sense
    Unhaunted quite of all but——nothingness?

III

A third time came they by;——alas! wherefore?
  My sleep had been embroider'd with dim dreams;
My soul had been a lawn besprinkled o'er
  With flowers, and stirring shades, and baffled beams:
The morn was clouded, but no shower fell,
    Tho' in her lids hung the sweet tears of May;
    The open casement press'd a new-leav'd vine,
Let in the budding warmth and throstle's lay;
    O Shadows! 'twas a time to bid farewell!
    Upon your skirts had fallen no tears of mine.

IV

A third time pass'd they by, and, passing, turn'd
  Each one the face a moment whiles to me;
Then faded, and to follow them I burn'd
  And ached for wings because I knew the three;
The first was a fair Maid, and Love her name;
    The second was Ambition, pale of cheek,
    And ever watchful with fatigued eye;
The last, whom I love more, the more of blame
    Is heap'd upon her, maiden most unmeek,——
    I knew to be my demon Poesy.

V

They faded, and forsooth! I wanted wings;
   O folly! What is Love! and where is it?
And for that poor Ambition——it springs
   From a man's little heart's short fever-fit;
For Poesy!——no,——she has not a joy,——
   At least for me,——so sweet as drowsy noons,
     And evenings steep'd in honied indolence;
O, for an age so shelter'd from annoy,
    That I may never know how change the moons,
    Or hear the voice of busy common-sense!

VI

So, ye three Ghosts, adieu! Ye cannot raise
   My head cool-bedded in the flowery grass;
For I would not be dieted with praise,
   A pet-lamb in a sentimental farce!
Fade softly from my eyes, and be once more
   In masque-like figures on the dreamy urn;
    Farewell! I yet have visions for the night,
And for the day faint visions there is store;
    Vanish, ye Phantoms! from my idle spright,
    Into the clouds, and never more return!

Sonnet

THE day is gone, and all its sweets are gone!
   Sweet voice, sweet lips, soft hand, and softer breast,
Warm breath, light whisper, tender semi-tone,
   Bright eyes, accomplish'd shape, and lang'rous waist!
Faded the flower and all its budded charms,
   Faded the sight of beauty from my eyes,
Faded the shape of beauty from my arms,
   Faded the voice, warmth, whiteness, paradise—
Vanish'd unseasonably at shut of eve,
   When the dusk holiday—or holinight
Of fragrant-curtain'd love begins to weave
   The woof of darkness thick, for hid delight;
But, as I've read love's missal through to-day,
   He'll let me sleep, seeing I fast and pray.

To – [Fanny]

I

WHAT can I do to drive away
Remembrance from my eyes? for they have seen,
Aye, an hour ago, my brilliant Queen!
Touch has a memory. O say, love, say,
What can I do to kill it and be free
In my old liberty?
When every fair one that I saw was fair,
Enough to catch me in but half a snare,
Not keep me there:
When, howe'er poor or particolour'd things,
My muse had wings,
And ever ready was to take her course
Whither I bent her force,
Unintellectual, yet divine to me;——
Divine, I say!——What sea-bird o'er the sea
Is a philosopher the while he goes
Winging along where the great water throes?

II

How shall I do
To get anew
Those moulted feathers, and so mount once more
Above, above
The reach of fluttering Love,
And make him cower lowly while I soar?
Shall I gulp wine? No, that is vulgarism,
A heresy and schism,
Foisted into the canon law of love;——
No,——wine is only sweet to happy men;
More dismal cares
Seize on me unawares,——

Where shall I learn to get my peace again?
To banish thoughts of that most hateful land,
Dungeoner of my friends, that wicked strand
Where they were wreck'd and live a wrecked life;
That monstrous region, whose dull rivers pour,
Ever from their sordid urns unto the shore,
Unown'd of any weedy-haired gods;
Whose winds, all zephyrless, hold scourging rods,
Iced in the great lakes, to afflict mankind;
Whose rank-grown forests, frosted, black, and blind,
Would fright a Dryad; whose harsh herbag'd meads
Make lean and lank the starv'd ox while he feeds;
There bad flowers have no scent, birds no sweet song,
And great unerring Nature once seem wrong.

III

O, for some sunny spell
To dissipate the shadows of this hell!
Say they are gone,——with the new dawning light
Steps forth my lady bright!
O, let me once more rest
My soul upon that dazzling breast!
Let once again these aching arms be plac'd,
The tender gaolers of thy waist!
And let me feel that warm breath here and there
To spread a rapture in my very hair,——
O, the sweetness of the pain!
Give me those lips again!
Enough! Enough! it is enough for me
To dream of thee!

Sonnet

I CRY your mercy——pity——love!——aye, love!
    Merciful love that tantalises not,
One-thoughted, never-wandering, guileless love,
    Unmask'd, and being seen——without a blot!
O! let me have thee whole,——all——all——be mine!
    That shápe, that fairness, that sweet minor zest
Of love, your kiss,——those hands, those eyes divine,
    That warm, white, lucent, million-pleasured breast,——
Yourself——your soul——in pity give me all,
    Withhold no atom's atom or I die,
Or living on perhaps, your wretched thrall,
    Forget, in the mist of idle misery,
Life's purposes,——the palate of my mind
    Losing its gust, and my ambition blind!

This Living Hand, Now Warm and Capable

THIS living hand, now warm and capable
Of earnest grasping, would, if it were cold
And in the icy silence of the tomb,
So haunt thy days and chill thy dreaming nights
That thou wouldst wish thine own heart dry of blood
So in my veins red life might stream again,
And thou be conscience-calm'd——see here it is——
I hold it towards you.

Bright Star

BRIGHT star! would I were steadfast as thou art——
    Not in lone splendour hung aloft the night
And watching, with eternal lids apart,
    Like nature's patient, sleepless Eremite,
The moving waters at their priestlike task
    Of pure ablution round earth's human shores,
Or gazing on the new soft fallen mask
    Or snow upon the mountains and the moors——
No——yet still steadfast, still unchangeable,
    Pillow'd upon my fair love's ripening breast,
To feel for ever its soft fall and swell,
    Awake for ever in a sweet unrest,
Still, still to hear her tender-taken breath,
And so live ever——or else swoon to death.

Ode to Fanny

I

PHYSICIAN Nature! let my spirit blood!
   O ease my heart of verse and let me rest;
Throw me upon thy Tripod, till the flood
   Of stifling numbers ebbs from my full breast.
A theme! a theme! great Nature! give a theme;
     Let me begin my dream.
I come——I see thee, as thou standest there,
Beckon me out into the wintry air.

II

Ah! dearest love, sweet home of all my fears,
   And hopes, and joys, and panting miseries,——
To-night, if I may guess, thy beauty wears
     A smile of such delight,
     As brilliant and as bright,
   As when with ravished, aching, vassal eyes,
     Lost in soft amaze,
     I gaze, I gaze!

III

Who now, with greedy looks, eats up my feast?
   What stare outfaces now my silver moon!
Ah! keep that hand unravished at the least;
     Let, let, the amorous burn——
     But, pr'ythee, do not turn
   The current of your heart from me so soon.
     O! save, in charity,
     The quickest pulse for me.

IV

Save it for me, sweet love! though music breathe
  Voluptuous visions into the warm air;
Though swimming through the dance's dangerous wreath;
    Be like an April day,
    Smiling and cold and gay,
  A temperate lily, temperate as fair;
    Then, Heaven! there will be
    A warmer June for me.

V

Why, this——you'll say, my Fanny! is not true:
  Put your soft hand upon your snowy side,
Where the heart beats: confess——'tis nothing new——
    Must not a woman be
    A feather on the sea,
  Sway'd to and fro by every wind and tide?
    Of as uncertain speed
    As blow-ball from the mead?

VI

I know it——and to know it is despair
  To one who loves you as I love, sweet Fanny!
Whose heart goes fluttering for you every where,
    Nor, when away you roam,
    Dare keep its wretched home,
  Love, Love alone, has pains severe and many:
    Then, loveliest! keep me free
    From torturing jealousy.

VII

Ah! if you prize my subdued soul above
  The poor, the fading, brief, pride of an hour;
Let none profane my Holy See of love,
    Or with a rude hand break
    The sacramental cake:
Let none else touch the just new-budded flower;
    If not——may my eyes close,
    Love! on their last repose.

In After-time, A Sage of Mickle Lore

In after-time, a sage of mickle lore
Yclep'd Typographus, the Giant took,
And did refit his limbs as heretofore,
And made him read in many a learned book,
And into many a lively legend look;
Thereby in goodly themes so training him,
That all his brutishness he quite forsook,
When, meeting Artegall and Talus grim,
    The one he struck stone-blind, the other's eyes wox dim.